9.7 1 pt.

DISCARD

The Guggenheim Museum Bilbao

by Sudipta Bardhan-Quallen

THOMSON
GALE

San Diego • Detroit • New York • San Francisco • Cleveland • New Haven, Conn. • Waterville, Maine • London • Munich

© 2004 by Blackbirch Press®. Blackbirch Press® is an imprint of Thomson Gale, a part of the Thomson Corporation.

Thomson is a trademark and Gale [and Blackbirch Press] are registered trademarks used herein under license.

For more information, contact
The Gale Group, Inc.
27500 Drake Rd.
Farmington Hills, MI 48331-3535
Or you can visit our Internet site at http://www.gale.com

ALL RIGHTS RESERVED
No part of this work covered by the copyright hereon may be reproduced or used in any form or by any means—graphic, electronic, or mechanical, including photocopying, recording, taping, Web distribution or information storage retrieval systems—without the written permission of the publisher.

Every effort has been made to trace the owners of copyrighted material.

Photo credits: cover © Jose Fusta Raga/ CORBIS; pages 4, 2, 381 © Donald Klein/ Super Stock; page 6 © Corel; page 7 © Oliver Strewe/ Lonely Planet Images; page 8 © Tim Hursley/ Super Stock; pages 10, 35 © Pavlovsky Jacques/ CORBIS SYGMA; page 11© Txema Fernandez/EPA/Landov; page 12 © Jacques M. Chenet / CORBIS; page 14 © Richard Cummins/ CORBIS; pages 15, 18, 22, 25, 27, 28, 34 © FMGB Guggenheim Bilbao Museoa, USA, 2004. Photograph by Erika Barahona Ede. All rights reserved. Total or partial reproduction prohibited; page 16 © Richard Schulman/ CORBIS; page 30 © Ben Wood/ CORBIS; page 32 © Ken Lucas/ Visuals Unlimited; page 36 © Associated Press, AP/ Javier Bauluz; page 40 © Tim Hursley/ Super Stock; page 42 © Douglas Peebles/ CORBIS

LIBRARY OF CONGRESS CATALOGING-IN-PUBLICATION DATA

Bardhan-Quallen, Sudipta
   The Guggenheim Museum Bilbao / by Sudipta Bardhan-Quallen.
      p. cm. — (Building world landmarks)
   Summary: Discusses the social and economic forces resulting in the decision to build the Guggenheim Museum Bilbao and the construction itself.
   ISBN 1-4103-0139-7 (hardback : alk. paper)

Printed in the United States
10 9 8 7 6 5 4 3 2 1

Table of Contents

Introduction
Architecture for Art's Sake 5

Chapter 1
A New Lease on Life 9

Chapter 2
Making Plans 17

Chapter 3
Details, Details 23

Chapter 4
The Making of an Icon 31

Chapter 5
The Miracle 39

Notes 44

Chronology 45

Glossary 46

For More Information 47

Index 48

Introduction

Architecture for Art's Sake

THE GUGGENHEIM MUSEUM Bilbao has been likened to everything from a titanium artichoke to an intergalactic spaceship to a metal flower. The architect of the building, Frank Owen Gehry, often says his intention was to create a cityscape like the kind found in science-fiction novels. Gehry's design for the museum exceeded all expectations and went beyond anything the world had ever seen before. In fact, his imaginative creation is as much of a draw for tourists as the art contained within.

Architecturally, the Guggenheim Museum Bilbao is often compared to the flagship of the Guggenheim Foundation, Frank Lloyd Wright's towering central atrium of the Solomon R. Guggenheim Museum in New York. Where Wright's design is somewhat problematic for practical concerns of museum curators—its

Opposite:
The Guggenheim Museum Bilbao has drawn more than a million visitors every year since it opened in 1997.

spiral exhibition ramp limits the display space available for artwork—Gehry's design does not sacrifice practicality for architectural beauty.

Nevertheless, the Guggenheim Museum Bilbao is every bit as iconic as Wright's building. With the museum as a backdrop, television commercials and music videos are filmed in Bilbao. Top designers transform the atrium into a catwalk for their fashion shows. Overall, more than a million people visit the museum every year—many of whom travel from great distances mainly to see the building.

Frank Lloyd Wright designed the Solomon R. Guggenheim Museum in New York City.

In many ways, Gehry's museum design has changed the way people approach architecture. Juan Ignacio Vidarte, the director of the Guggenheim Museum Bilbao, has said of the project: "We wanted this building to be of the same quality as its contents, with an importance equal to that of the artworks it would eventually house. Over these years, I have been pleased, and to a certain extent astonished, to see the actual project exceeding our ambitions."[1]

The iconic architecture of the Guggenheim Museum Bilbao has become as visually important as the works of art it houses.

Chapter 1

A New Lease on Life

THE CITY OF Bilbao, in the Basque region of Spain, was founded in the year 1300. Originally, Bilbao was a seaport and an ironworking settlement. Over time, it became a flourishing industrial port. The city's riverside location and valuable natural resources enabled shipbuilding, mining, and steel manufacturing to become major industries almost immediately. In 1511, the city's importance as a business center was established with the founding of a trade consulate, a place for representatives from the various regions and countries that traded with Spain to meet and discuss commercial matters. Although its economic success peaked during the Industrial Revolution of the 1800s, for centuries Bilbao was the industrial capital of the region and eventually grew to be the fourth-largest city in Spain.

Opposite:
During the 1990s, the Guggenheim Museum Bilbao (foreground) was part of a massive revitalization of the city of Bilbao, the fourth-largest city in Spain.

Hard Times, Hard Decisions

By the 1980s, however, Bilbao's economy was faltering. The steel mills and the shipyards were closing. Unemployment was so high that one out of five workers was out of a job. Economic hard times threatened the future prosperity of Bilbao and its four hundred thousand residents.

In 1991, government officials in Bilbao set a $1.5 billion budget to finance a number of major renovations intended to revitalize the city. In the plans were an expansion of the airport, including a new terminal and control tower, a new conference and performing arts center, and a new subway system. The centerpiece of the urban revitalization would be a cultural center to display contemporary art.

There were two problems with the planned centerpiece. The first was that no one in Bilbao had the expertise to run a museum that held internationally famous artwork. The second problem was that the Basques did not own a collection of artwork that would draw tourists from all over the world.

As a solution, the Basque officials contacted the Solomon R. Guggenheim Foundation and proposed a partnership. Bilbao

Located on the Nervión River, Bilbao was once a major seaport and shipping center.

A Brief History of the Basques

For hundreds of years, the people of the Basque region considered themselves a separate community from neighboring nations, including Spain. They had their own customs, traditions, and even a language called Euskara that bore no resemblance to Spanish. In 1833, during the First Carlist War in Spain, the Basque provinces of Vizcaya, Alava, and Guipuzcoa supported the Carlists against the Spanish central government. When the Carlists were defeated in 1839, the Basques entered into a treaty with the government that made the provinces a part of Spain but with the right to govern themselves.

During the Second Carlist War, which broke out in 1872, the Basque provinces again sided against the Spanish central government. When the Carlists were defeated a second time in 1876, the Basques lost their rights of self-government.

Finally, during the Spanish Civil War

The people of the Basque Country in Spain have their own unique traditions, language, and governmental bodies.

in 1936, an independent Basque republic was established. The newly created Euskadi (or Basque Country) would still be considered a part of Spain, but would be autonomous in many ways. It issued its own currency and passports, set up its own judiciary, established diplomatic links with several foreign countries, and organized its own army. Since democracy arrived in Spain in the late 1970s, Euskadi has had its own parliament.

would provide an old 257,000-square-foot (23,876 square meters) wine-storage warehouse called the Alhóndiga to be the site of a new art museum. In addition, Bilbao promised $100 million in financing. The Guggenheim Foundation would provide the art and the expertise to run a world-class museum.

An Interesting Proposal

At first, Guggenheim director Thomas Krens was not sure about building a Guggenheim museum in Bilbao. He was not worried that Bilbao was too out-of-the-way for the kind of museum the Basques wanted; Krens believed that "if the art is significant, people will come to see it, make a pilgrimage to it."[2] His biggest concern was actually the Alhóndiga site itself.

Guggenheim director Thomas Krens believed that people would travel to Bilbao if its new museum held internationally famous art.

The Basques had originally proposed that Alhóndiga be modified to house the art museum. According to Krens, "They [the Basque officials] planned to leave the exterior skirt [the low outer walls surrounding the original building] . . . and just destroy the whole interior of the building."[3] Inside the exterior skirt, a high glass box could be built to serve as the museum. In the minds of the Basque officials, renovating the

Alhóndiga in such a way would serve dual purposes—an old landmark would get a new lease on life, and a new cultural attraction would be created in Bilbao.

For Krens and the Guggenheim representatives, however, the site had many drawbacks. There were dozens of interior columns spaced closely together. These would get in the way of building large gallery spaces. In addition, the ceilings were quite low, which would limit the size of the display pieces. Krens knew "the only way you could do a great building was to have a great site."[4] He decided that he needed an architect's perspective to confirm his belief that the Alhóndiga was not a feasible museum site. He invited Frank Owen Gehry to come to Bilbao to give his opinion.

A New Perspective

Krens had previously worked with Gehry in 1988. At that time, the two had teamed up to transform a factory in North Adams, Massachusetts, into the Massachusetts Museum of Contemporary Art. Since Gehry had a reputation for transforming industrial spaces into architectural masterpieces, Krens felt confident that the architect's opinion would be valuable.

On May 20, 1991, Gehry arrived in Bilbao. He examined the Alhóndiga and its surrounding areas. Almost immediately, he concluded that the Alhóndiga would not be the best site for the proposed art museum. He knew that the Basque government was trying to redevelop the area around the Nervión River, so he suggested that as an alternative. He, as well as Krens, felt that the presence of the Bellas Artes

Frank O. Gehry

Frank Gehry was born in Toronto, Canada, on February 28, 1929. He spent much of his time as a child in his grandfather's hardware store, where he played with nails, screws, and pipes and learned to cut glass and metal. From an early age, he became interested in construction and in the beauty of different materials. After his family moved to Los Angeles, Gehry took a class in architecture. The subject made a lasting impression on Gehry.

Gehry studied architecture at the University of Southern California and then studied urban planning at the Graduate School of Design at Harvard. After working for various architectural firms, he established his own firm, Frank O. Gehry and Associates, in 1963.

Over the years, Gehry has designed a number of high-profile buildings. Many elements he explored in early buildings came together in the design for the Guggenheim Museum Bilbao. For example, fishlike scales appear in many of Gehry's earlier works, including Fishdance restaurant in Kobe, Japan, and the highly abstract fish sculpture Gehry created for the 1992 Barcelona Olympic Games. Metal exteriors appear in Gehry's design of the Frederick R. Weisman Museum in Minneapolis, Minnesota. The irregular, flower-

The metal exteriors of Frank Gehry's Frederick P. Weisman Museum (pictured) in Minneapolis are similar to those of the Guggenheim Museum Bilbao.

petal skylights that top the Guggenheim Museum Bilbao were recycled from a proposal Gehry designed for the Los Angeles Rapid Transit District Tower.

The Guggenheim Museum Bilbao was such an architectural success that many people consider it to be Gehry's masterpiece. Even at the museum's completion, however, Gehry, then aged sixty-eight, showed no sign of slowing down. In fact, he followed up on the success of Bilbao with the completion of the Experience Music Project building in Seattle, Washington, in 2000 and the Walt Disney Concert Hall in Los Angeles, California, in 2003.

Gehry approved of this site at the bend of the Nervión River, where an abandoned lumber mill once stood, as the future home of the Guggenheim Museum Bilbao.

Museum, the Teatro Arriaga opera house, and the Deusto University made the riverside the true cultural center of Bilbao.

At first, the Basque government was concerned by the idea of a change of venue. Much of the riverside was privately owned. Other portions were owned by the Spanish government. They worried that they would not be able to find a site along the river to meet the expectations of the Guggenheim Foundation. As it turned out, however, a piece of land on the bend of the river that housed an abandoned lumber mill was available. After some discussion, a decision was made: the Guggenheim Museum Bilbao would be built between two bridges, the Puente de la Salve and the Puente de Deusto, on the banks of the Nervión River. The site was pleasing to all, and especially to Gehry, who later wrote: "To be at the bend of a working river intersected by a large bridge, and connecting the urban fabric of a fairly dense city to the river's edge with a place for modern art is my idea of heaven."[5]

Chapter 2

Making Plans

ONCE AN ARRANGEMENT was reached between the Basque government and the Guggenheim Foundation, the search began to find an architect who would design a building that, as Krens later explained, "captured the public imagination . . . and [would come] to symbolize the city."[6] Heinrich Klotz of Frankfurt, Germany, a specialist in contemporary architecture, was asked to act as an adviser in the selection process, and Krens was asked to recommend three prospective architects—a European architect, an Asian architect, and an American architect. The competition was held between Coop Himmelblau, Arata Isozaki, and Frank Gehry. Each was invited to come up with a presentation that would portray their vision of the museum.

The Guggenheim Museum Bilbao had unique requirements for the museum world because the

Opposite:
Gehry, pictured here in his studio, won the international competition to find an architect whose design would complement the existing cityscape and be an icon on its own.

The executive committee wanted the museum to complement the existing cityscape and incorporate the Puente de la Salve, the bridge on the east end of the site (pictured).

planners wanted proportionally more gallery space than in traditional museums. Since the Bilbao museum was partnered with the Guggenheim Foundation, it could share resources with the Guggenheim museums in New York—and because of this, would need less space for offices and other nondisplay areas. In their designs, the architects would have to maximize the gallery space. In addition, the building they envisioned would have to complement the existing cityscape near the proposed site. Some of the elements that would have to be incorporated included the Puente de la Salve that lay to the east, the historic Muelle de Evaristo Churruca road that ran along the riverfront to the north, and the buildings on the Alameda de Mazarredo that lay to the south.

Alternate Proposals

By July 20, 1991, all of the proposals had arrived at the Frankfurter Hof Hotel in Frankfurt, where they would be considered by an executive committee. Isozaki's sketches showed his plans to build a conservative oval-shaped structure, but his proposal did not include a strong connection to the Puente de la Salve. The executive committee felt that the bridge should be an important part of the overall plan, so Isozaki's proposal was rejected.

Coop Himmelblau proposed a design that used both sides as well as the space beneath the Puente de la Salve. As a way to link Bilbao's past to its future, it also preserved the old lumber mill with its smokestack that sat on the site. The design included a number of differently shaped galleries suspended inside box-shaped buildings coated in translucent skin. At night, the skin would seem to disappear, which would create the illusion of galleries suspended in air.

The executive committee, however, was concerned that the simple box shapes in the Coop Himmelblau model would not create the type of architectural presence they dreamed of. They were looking for a design that would have a greater visual impact than what Coop Himmelblau had envisioned. The committee members then turned their attention to Gehry's proposal.

The Winner

Although Gehry had seen the site back in May, he did not begin to sketch his ideas until he and the other candidates visited Bilbao in late June and early July. He had noticed that the waterfront had an industrial feel, and he wanted to create a design that preserved that aspect of Bilbao. He was determined that his building would link the city on the plateau above to the incline toward the river with a strong visual presence.

Gehry did not, however, immediately know how he wanted the museum to look. His first ideas included three rectangular floors stacked cleanly, an octagon of tapering floor sizes, and a ziggurat (a pyramid made from a stack of successively smaller stories), all surrounded by smaller rooms to serve as restaurants or other museum facilities. These ideas quickly evolved into a rectangular structure with several tapering floors, topped by sail-like shapes to add embellishment to the building.

None of these seemed perfect, however. Since the site was on the waterfront, Gehry liked the idea of some sort of nautical theme. He came up with several to experiment with: the shape of a ship's bow, the scales of a fish, and the undulations of waves. To expand on this theme, he had the idea of an ocean-liner shape for the main gallery. Gehry also wanted to avoid conventional squares and rectangles for skylights, so he began to design wavy, irregular shapes. He laid metal model pieces on a cityscape of Bilbao he had in his office. Slowly, the idea developed that, from above, the building should look like a flower. The main museum lay on one side of the Puente de la Salve; on the other side of the bridge, Gehry laid the plans for a tower that would overlook the river. A long gallery running under the bridge would act as a base for the tower and also serve to connect the main building to the tower.

Gehry's final design could be described as a futuristic vessel clad in metal. The central rotunda would rise to a height of 165 feet (38.1 meters), and the main gallery, which extended under the Puente de la Salve, would be longer than a football field.  The museum's three levels would be stacked to give a silhouette that resembled a ship, topped by a metal roof that Gehry designed to be both irregular and sculptural. In fact, very few of the surfaces in Gehry's proposal were not irregular—from the walls of the galleries to the arches of the atrium, the museum would be made of complex curves and arcs. The use of limestone, steel, and glass on the exteriors gave the design a rugged, industrial feel—Gehry's tribute to Bilbao's history.

The final design that made its way to Frankfurt from Gehry was certainly unique; most of the selection committee felt that the building Gehry proposed would be an icon all on its own. They gambled that people would want to visit Gehry's building as much as they wanted to see the artwork inside. The day after the committee began to evaluate proposals, Gehry was officially selected to be the architect of the Guggenheim Museum Bilbao.

Gehry's final design included a gallery that runs under the Puente de la Salve to connect the main building of the museum to a tower overlooking the river.

Chapter 3

Details, Details

FROM THE BEGINNING, it was clear that building the complex shapes in Gehry's plans would be a huge undertaking. The design competition only laid out general plans for the museum. After Gehry had won, all the details had to be worked out. He and his team of architects began work immediately.

Parallel Planning

Representatives of the Basque government felt strongly that Gehry should have as much freedom as possible to create the building he had envisioned. They felt equally strongly, however, that the project be completed on time and within the budget. Gehry was designated the design architect, but another company called IDOM was given the role of executive architect. IDOM was ultimately responsible for

Opposite:
Building the complex geometric shapes Gehry envisioned for the Guggenheim Museum Bilbao required a lot of careful planning.

making sure the construction of the museum progressed acceptably. In fact, once a target cost had been approved by the Basques, an agreement was put into place that created a financial penalty for IDOM should the cost of construction exceed the target cost.

Throughout the design and construction processes, a new cost estimate was produced every six weeks. This ensured that architects and engineers made informed decisions about plan changes and kept budget and timetable in mind.

The leaders in the Basque government who supported the idea of a Guggenheim museum in Bilbao were also very anxious for construction to get under way as soon as possible. Since the financing was coming from public funds, support for the museum was somewhat dependent on the results of the next election—if representatives who did not support the construction of the museum were to be elected, funding could be withdrawn by a new administration. To prevent the possibility that the project would become an election issue, the leaders in office wanted construction to begin before the Basque regional fall 1994 elections. This course of action all but ensured that the museum would be built.

By January 1993, however, the Guggenheim Museum Bilbao project was still in the schematic design phase. It was estimated that more than one thousand detail drawings would be needed to properly build such a complex building, but only thirty of these drawings had been completed so far. This development phase was scheduled to take two years or more.

This, in turn, meant that construction could not begin until 1995, and the museum would probably not be completed on time.

To avoid delays, it was decided that some construction would begin even before the designs were finalized. Tasks like the demolition of existing structures on the proposed museum site could be started before the final details of the building were decided upon. Gehry agreed to this arrangement, and in October 1993, demolition began and plans for the museum's foundation were developed.

The Nervión River posed a problem for the foundation design of the Guggenheim Museum Bilbao.

In late 1993, while the building plans were still being developed, site preparation began with the demolition of abandoned buildings.

Since the site was so close to the river, the foundation would have to be built on land prone to shifting. There was also a real possibility of flooding at some point in the future. A flood could do millions of dollars of damage to—or even destroy—the artwork that would be displayed in the museum. To prevent flood damage to the museum, the foundation was built with "water anchors" that would hold the building in place in the event of a flood. A total of 664 holes were drilled into the bedrock to accommodate steel cables. These cables were held in place by concrete and were used to anchor the building to the site. As an extra precaution against water damage, all the artwork displayed in the building would be hung above the five-hundred-year flood level.

Gehry and CATIA

While the foundation was being laid, Gehry needed to figure out how to translate his complex geometric shapes into an architectural reality. To accomplish this goal, Gehry and his team turned to CATIA (Computer Aided Three-dimensional Interactive Application), a computer program that was developed for the aerospace industry.

When Gehry first showed his plans for the museum to contractors and manufacturers, he was often told that his unusual shapes and sculptural forms either could not be built or would be too expensive to build. Using CATIA, however, Gehry's associate Jim Glymph thought he could computerize all of the plans for the Guggenhcim Museum Bilbao. The computer

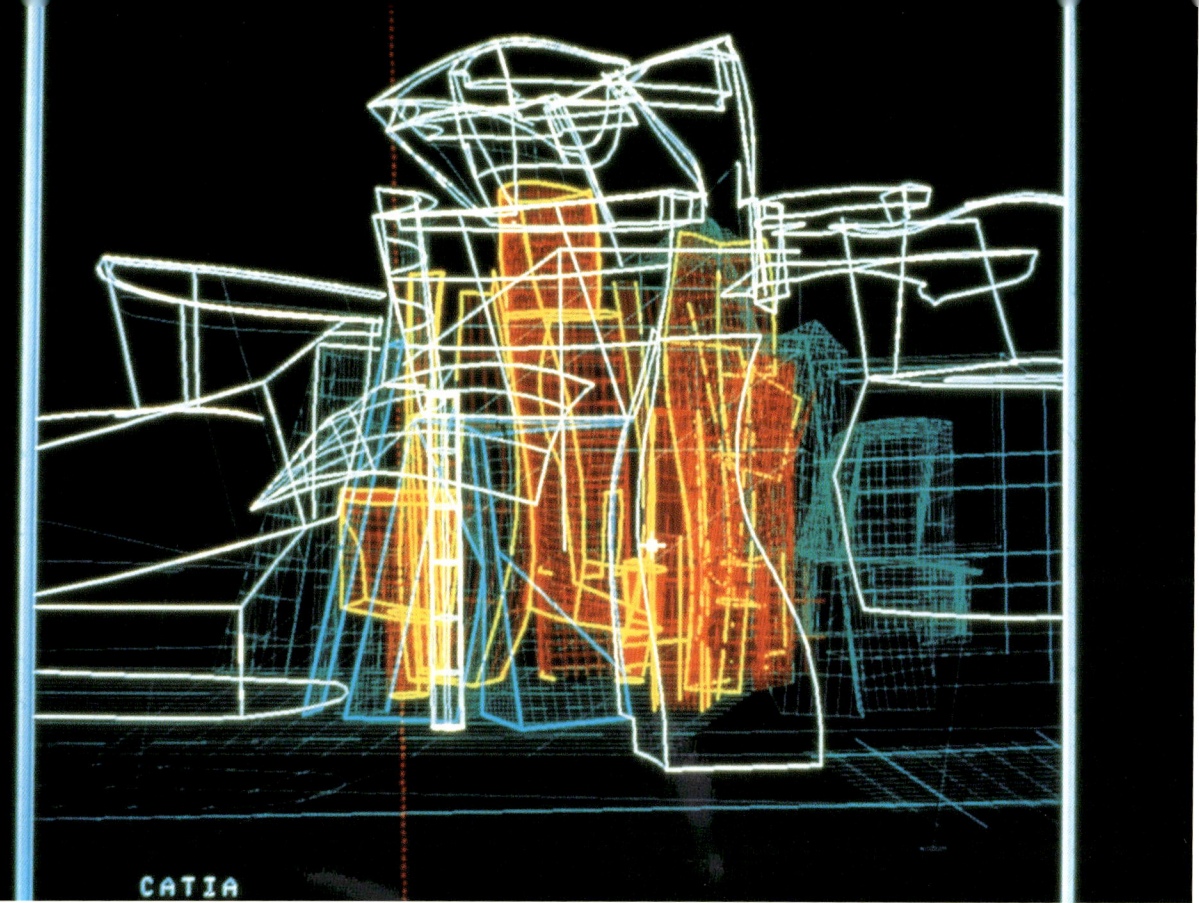

could figure out whether the pieces were feasible or not with far more accuracy than its human counterparts.

At first, Gehry was very resistant to using a computer program to aid in the design. "I just didn't like the images of the computer,"[7] Gehry explains. Glymph and his team had to hide the machines that ran CATIA in a corner of the office, out of sight, since Gehry did not want to see them.

Soon, however, CATIA's value to the design process became clear, and Gehry's attitude changed. CATIA was able to produce detailed plans on how to build every panel, piece, and part of the building. Based on these plans, a scale model was first built out of foam. When the model was successfully built, the information from

All of Gehry's building plans were computerized using the CATIA program, which prevented expensive and time-consuming errors.

The structural framework of the Guggenheim Museum Bilbao was made up of three layers of steel: a grid made of girders, a layer of horizontal tubes, and a layer of vertical tubes.

CATIA was used to assemble the steel structures for the building and to mill the limestone panels.

The use of CATIA dramatically changed the design process for the Guggenheim Museum Bilbao. Said Glymph, "Prior to the development of computer applications in the office, [Gehry's plans for the Bilbao museum] would have been considered something to move away from. It might have been a sketch idea, but we would never be able to build it."[8] CATIA made the museum possible because it was able to generate precise specifications for contractors to follow, and it spotted potential obstacles long before the construction phase. If a certain structure was not practical to build, CATIA identified the problems early on. Gehry could then make adjustments to correct the problems.

By using CATIA, expensive and time-consuming errors were avoided.

A Solid Structure

While Gehry's team used CATIA to iron out the details, construction on the building's foundation continued until April 1995. Work on the building's steel structure, however, began in September 1994. Once again, overlapping two phases of the project helped keep everything on schedule.

The structural framework for the museum building consisted of three layers of steel connected by high-strength bolts. The innermost layer was a grid of nine-square-foot sections made of steel girders. This layer was designed to create a boxlike skeleton for each piece of the building. The building's curvature was not established in the first structural layer—instead, the second and third layers that lay on top of the grid formed the basis for the curves and bends.

The second layer consisted of galvanized steel tubes that ran horizontally at nine-foot (2.75 meters) intervals; the third layer was identical except that the tubes ran vertically. The tubes in these layers were rounded and bent to match the curvature Gehry planned for the exterior of the building. Finally, a layer of galvanized steel was bolted to the frames as a surface on which the outer skin could be attached.

Approximately $22 million was spent on the structure alone. As the structural frame approached completion, Gehry's vision began to take shape. The sculptural forms in his plans were an imminent reality.

Chapter 4

The Making of an Icon

As soon as the structural work on the building was completed, the exteriors could be applied. The planned exteriors of the Guggenheim Museum Bilbao were extremely complex—metal and stone panels sculpted into various curving forms, as well as twenty-two hundred glass panels. In addition to finding materials that fit Gehry's aesthetic vision, the cost of the materials had to fit the project budget.

The Beauty of Titanium

Gehry's original idea for the building incorporated a metal skin made from hand-polished stainless steel. This skin would be for aesthetic purposes only, as the building already had a structural layer of steel as part of the frame. Gehry felt, however, that polished metal on the exterior of the museum would add to the

Opposite:
More than 270,000 square feet of titanium make up the shiny metal skin of the Guggenheim Museum Bilbao.

Russia, one of the two places titanium ore (pictured) is mined, began to liquidate titanium stocks at the same time the Guggenheim Museum Bilbao wanted to purchase the metal.

industrial feel of the building, which was an essential part of his design.

After the design competition, however, Gehry decided that he did not like the way this particular metal looked. He felt that stainless steel shone too brightly in full sunlight and was too dull in cloudy weather. He considered leaded copper as an alternative, but was advised against using it. Leaded copper posed a toxicity risk, since the rainy climate in Bilbao could wash lead from the skin into the environment.

Gehry came across the possibility of using titanium for the metal skin almost by accident. He received a promotional sample of titanium from a vendor, and he realized that titanium would be perfect. Explains

Gehry, "Titanium was so beautiful in the Bilbao light, and it actually turns gold in the rain."[9]

Because titanium is very rare—it is only mined in Australia and Russia—it is usually much more expensive than stainless steel or leaded copper. Gehry feared it would be too costly to purchase the more than 270,000 square feet (82,297 meters) of metal it would take to cover the building.

Through a lucky coincidence, the world's largest titanium manufacturer, Russia, began to liquidate its titanium stocks at precisely the time that the Guggenheim Museum Bilbao wanted to purchase this metal. The huge influx of titanium lowered the price dramatically. Within a week of the prices dropping, Gehry had purchased enough titanium to complete his building. The purchase was so large that the market was no longer flooded with titanium; as a result, the price went back up to the original levels.

The titanium had to be chemically treated and laminated before it could be used on the building. The treated titanium was then cut into 42,875 panels and shipped to the construction site. In addition to it being harder than stainless steel, titanium presents a number of other benefits. For example, the melting point of titanium is three thousand degrees Fahrenheit—meaning the metal skin is essentially fireproof. This aspect increases the durability of the exterior of the museum.

Titanium is also an extremely lightweight metal. A single installer could comfortably handle each panel, and the panels were installed one by one. The light

Plans for the exterior included metal and stone panels as well as twenty-two hundred glass panels.

weight of the panels became important because of the way the building curved. There were numerous areas that were inaccessible by cranes, so the construction companies had to hire climbers to rappel down the sides of the building and fix the panels into place with three clamps on each side. Said Rodríguez Llopis, an engineer involved in the Bilbao project: "We found that it was easier to hire climbers and train them as crimpers [the technicians that would affix the metal panels to the building] than to hire crimpers and train them as climbers."[10]

Since Gehry did not want the metal skin of the building to appear too high tech, applying the titanium

panels by hand gave them soft bends and dents. When clamped in place, the panels have a more handmade appearance. In addition, since the titanium is quite thin—at only 0.015 inch (0.4 millimeter) thick, it is approximately the thickness of four sheets of paper— and only clamped at the edges, the panels flutter in the wind, which gives the exterior further texture.

Each of the 42,875 titanium panels was applied by hand and flutters in the wind, adding texture to the outside of the building.

In Search of Stone

Gehry also planned to use stone on the exterior of the Guggenheim Museum Bilbao. He wanted to find a beige limestone that would be strong enough to withstand Bilbao's humid and rainy weather conditions.

35

The museum's limestone exterior panels had natural color variations, so a technician had to arrange them by hand for the most visually pleasing effect.

In the design phase, Gehry had intended to use Spanish limestone for the museum. During the actual selection process, the first sample to appear appropriate for the job was called Caliza Santa. Further inquiry revealed, however, that this particular stone was quarried in a politically turbulent area of Israel. A continuous supply of it could not be guaranteed because of the upheaval in the region around the quarry.

Instead, Gehry managed to find a Spanish source for the limestone, from a quarry called Huéscar. The problem with this option, however, was that Huéscar had filed for bankruptcy. The qualities Gehry was looking for—a stone with low porosity and high density—made the stone too hard to cut or shape using conventional tools. As a result, Huéscar had been having a difficult time quarrying enough stone to turn a profit. The order placed by the Guggenheim Museum Bilbao—more than 44,450 cubic yards (34.000 cubic meters)—was enough to reopen the Huéscar quarry.

Since the stone was so hard, a machine that was normally used to mill metal was adapted to mill the limestone. It took a year just to make the necessary machine adjustments to be able to cut the stones chosen for the museum. The panels were eventually milled using information generated by the CATIA computer program. It took two years of working seven days a week, twenty-four hours a day, to finish cutting the limestone to the proper specifications.

Back at the construction site, the placement of each panel was determined by hand selection. Since the stone had natural color variations, a technician on site had to arrange the panels in a way that was visually pleasing. Finally, each panel was secured to the structure using clips specially manufactured to withstand the wind pressure, which can be greater than twenty-eight hundred pounds per square inch at the museum site.

By mid-1996, construction of the exterior of the Guggenheim Museum Bilbao was essentially completed, and work on the interior had been progressing since August 1995. Right on schedule, all construction was finished by October 1997.

Chapter 5

The Miracle

ON OCTOBER 18, Spain's King Juan Carlos opened the museum with the words: "The Guggenheim Museum is inaugurated!"[11] He flipped the master switch and illuminated the 165-foot- (50.3-meter-) high atrium at a gala attended by eight hundred international dignitaries.

Upon seeing Gehry's building completed, critics and admirers struggled for the words to describe it. "Miracle" was the most common praise. As visionary as the design was on paper, in real life the museum sparked discussion, debate, and, in the first months after opening, a desire on the part of hundreds of thousands of people to travel to Bilbao to see it.

The New Standard

The building itself, positioned on the banks of the Nervión River, looks like a futuristic ocean liner. The

Opposite:
Gehry designed the Guggenheim Museum Bilbao to project a futuristic nautical image that complements its location on the Nervión River.

The Guggenheim Museum Bilbao's nineteen galleries, many with curving and tilting walls, provide three levels of display space.

metal skin completes the nautical imagery by resembling thousands of fish scales that shimmer in the sunlight. The irregular skylights Gehry had envisioned crown the building like a titanium flower. An exterior water garden helps integrate the building with the riverside site.

Despite its strong visual impact, the museum does not clash with its surroundings. According to Guggenheim Museum Bilbao director Juan Ignacio Vidarte, the building "reacts very well to the urban environment, not trying to replicate it but on the other hand it looks familiar. It doesn't look odd although it's different."[12] The museum's connection to Bilbao, both visually and spiritually, was important to Gehry. As he later explained, "I spent a lot of time trying to understand the culture, trying to understand the people. . . . I can't put my finger on a piece of the building and say this is Basque, but they seem to think I captured their spirit."[13]

Inside, the nineteen galleries that are spread over three levels have a total of over 112,000 square feet (10,405 square meters) of display space. Ten of the galleries are rectangular, identifiable from the outside by their limestone coverings; the remaining nine galleries are irregularly shaped with bowing and tilting walls, and can be identified by their titanium skin. The largest of the galleries is known as "the boat"—at 450 feet (137.2 meters) long, it is the length of one and a half football fields. The boat is also 80 feet (24.4 meters) wide; the gallery is large enough to house a blue whale with room to spare. This gallery can be seen from the outside as the long section that runs under the Puente de la Salve to connect the main building to the tower on the other side.

In another architectural feat, the boat is free of any support columns. Gehry had planned to divide the spaces with interior walls, but Krens preferred that the space be left free for oversized works of art. The large uninterrupted floor of the boat has been appropriated for the thirteen-foot-tall and hundred-foot-long contemporary sculpture called *Snake* by Richard Serra. Without the Guggenheim Museum Bilbao and its extralarge galleries, this particular work of art could not be displayed anywhere.

A Popular Choice

The public opening took place the day after the formal ceremony, on October 19, 1997. In the first year that the Guggenheim Museum Bilbao was open to the public, 1.36 million people visited the museum. This

The Bilbao Effect

The Experience Music Project building (pictured) in Seattle is one of several buildings Gehry designed after the Guggenheim Museum Bilbao.

Frank Gehry's museum was such a success that other cities have included similar buildings as a part of their own revitalization plans. Eager to achieve what has become known as the "Bilbao effect," places like Seattle, Washington; Pittsburgh, Pennsylvania; and Denver, Colorado, have gambled that a similar phenomenon can take place in their own backyards. They are willing to pay high prices for world-renowned architects, all in the hopes that the miracle of Bilbao—and its multimillion-dollar impact on the local economy—will repeat itself. Often, they call on Gehry himself to re-create the magic.

It is unclear, however, whether the phenomenon that made the Guggenheim Museum Bilbao such a success can be easily repeated. Some things like the unique titanium skin are unlikely to be duplicated for economic reasons. Even another partnership between Gehry and the Guggenheim Foundation for a new museum in Manhattan, New York, failed to get enough public support for the project to move forward.

number was three times larger than the projections made during the planning stages of the museum. This influx of visitors has had a huge impact on the tourist industry in the city of Bilbao and in the Basque Country in general. The museum itself generated $198 million in tourism revenues in the first year alone, and an estimated 79 percent of the first year's visitors traveled to Bilbao primarily to see the Guggenheim. Even more remarkable is that approximately 15 percent of the Guggenheim Museum Bilbao's visitors had never been to a museum before.

The economic impact of the Guggenheim Museum Bilbao goes beyond the admission prices, hotel and restaurant revenues, and transportation profits. Many industries related to the construction of the building have profited from their association. For example, the Huéscar quarry has become famous for supplying the stone to the Bilbao museum. This fame has helped it stay open and profitable.

The popularity of the Guggenheim Museum Bilbao has not faded over time. Every year for the first five years after it opened, at least 1 million visitors arrived. Six out of every seven visitors come from outside the Basque region. Every year, the museum organizes new exhibits and acquires more artwork in an effort to keep the public interest high. Regardless of what is housed inside, the distinguishing architecture of the building itself stands as a global icon for a new millennium.

Notes

Introduction: Architecture for Art's Sake
1. Quoted in Frank O. Gehry and Coosje van Bruggen, *Frank O. Gehry: Guggenheim Museum Bilbao*. New York: Harry N. Abrams, 1999, p. 12.

Chapter 1: A New Lease on Life
2. Quoted in Gehry and van Bruggen, *Frank O. Gehry*, p. 19.
3. Quoted in Gehry and van Bruggen, *Frank O. Gehry*, p. 17.
4. Quoted in Gehry and van Bruggen, *Frank O. Gehry*, p. 24.
5. Quoted in Robert Hughes, "Bravo! Bravo!" *Time*, November 3, 1997.

Chapter 2: Making Plans
6. Quoted in PBS, "The Beauty of Basque," MacNeil/Lehrer NewsHour, October 21, 1997.

Chapter 3: Details, Details
7. Gehry and van Bruggen, *Frank O. Gehry*, p. 136.
8. Quoted in Gehry and van Bruggen, *Frank O. Gehry*, p. 138.

Chapter 4: The Making of an Icon
9. Quoted in PBS, "The Beauty of Basque."
10. Quoted in Francisco Gonzalez-Pulido, Pablo Vaggione, and Laura A. Ackley, "Managing the Construction of the Museo Guggenheim Bilbao," Center for Design Informatics at Harvard Design School, 2002. www.cdi.gsd.harvard.edu.

Chapter 5: The Miracle
11. Quoted in CNN, "Security Tight as Guggenheim Museum Opens in Basque City," October 18, 1997. www.cnn.com.
12. Quoted in CNN, "The 'Miracle' of the Guggenheim," November 19, 2002. www.cnn.com.
13. Quoted in PBS, "The Beauty of Basque."

Chronology

1991   The Basque Government plans $1.5 billion revitalization for the city of Bilbao and contacts the Solomon R. Guggenheim Foundation to help build a world-class museum.

May 20: Frank Gehry arrives in Bilbao to evaluate the Alhóndiga site; between Gehry and Thomas Krens, a recommendation is made to move the museum site to the banks of the Nervión River.

June 26: Krens invites Gehry, Arata Isozaki, and Coop Himmelblau to create designs for the prospective Guggenheim Museum Bilbao.

July 20: The proposals from all three architects arrive to be judged by an executive committee.

July 21: Gehry is selected to be the architect of the Guggenheim Museum Bilbao.

1993   October 20: Groundbreaking of the Guggenheim Museum Bilbao, demolition of existing structures on the site and the laying of the foundation for the new building begins.

1994   September: Construction of the building's steel structure begins.

1995   April: Work on the museum's exteriors begins.

August: Work on the museum's interiors begins.

1996   May: Construction of the exteriors is completed, detail work on the grounds of the building, including landscaping and construction of walkways, begins.

1997   October 18: The Guggenheim Museum Bilbao is opened by King Juan Carlos of Spain.

October 19: Public opening of the museum.

1998   November 2: A Guggenheim Foundation press release announces that 1.36 million people visited the Guggenheim Museum Bilbao in the first year.

2002   October 18: A Guggenheim Foundation report states that the Bilbao museum received more than 5.15 million visitors in the first five years.

Glossary

architect—a person trained to design buildings and other structures.

atrium—an open, central area, often with skylights, especially in public buildings.

Basque Country—area in northern Spain comprised of the provinces of Vizcaya, Álava, and Guipúzcoa.

CATIA—stands for Computer Aided Three-dimensional Interactive Application; a computer program that can produce building specifications for complex designs. CATIA was originally developed for the aerospace industry.

crimper—a technician who affixes metal panels to a building.

foundation—architecturally, the stone or concrete that underlies a structure to provide support.

Industrial Revolution—the term that refers to the social and economic changes that took place in the eighteenth century when home-based manufacturing was replaced with large-scale factory production.

leaded copper—an alloy of copper that includes lead.

limestone—a common rock used in construction.

quarry—a place where rock is excavated and harvested.

Solomon R. Guggenheim Foundation—a philanthropic foundation established by Solomon R. Guggenheim in 1937 aimed at supporting all forms of art.

titanium—an extremely strong elemental metal.

trade consulate—a place for representatives from various regions and countries to meet and discuss commercial matters.

Vizcaya province—the province within Basque Country where Bilbao is located.

water anchor—a special structure used in the foundations of buildings in areas of high flood risk that helps keep the foundation steady in the event of a flood.

ziggurat—a pyramid made from a stack of successively smaller stories.

For More Information

Books

Frank O. Gehry, Beatriz Colomina, Mildred Friedman, William J. Mitchell, J. Fiona Ragheb, and Jean-Louis Cohen, *Frank Gehry, Architect*. New York: Solomon R. Guggenheim Museum, 2001.

Frank O. Gehry and Coosje van Bruggen, *Frank O. Gehry: Guggenheim Museum Bilbao*. New York: Harry N. Abrams, 1999.

Mark Kurlansky, *The Basque History of the World*. New York: Penguin USA, 2001.

Periodicals

Robert Hughes, "Bravo! Bravo!" *Time*, November 3, 1997.

Cathleen McGuigan, "Basque-ing in Glory," *Newsweek*, January 13, 1997.

Peter Plagens, "Another Tale of Two Cities," *Newsweek*, November 3, 1997.

Web Sites

Bilbao(www.bilbao-city.net). Provides a history of the city of Bilbao and descriptions of the revitalization projects that are being undertaken, including the Guggenheim Museum Bilbao.

The Guggenheim Museum Bilbao (www.guggenheim-bilbao.es). Provides a history of the construction of the Guggenheim Museum Bilbao, as well as general descriptions of the museum and its collections.

The Solomon R. Guggenheim Foundation (www.guggenheim.org). Provides a history of the Guggenheim Foundation with information on the various museums worldwide.

Index

Alhóndiga, 12–13

Basques, 11, 24, 40
Bilbao, 9–10
Bilbao effect, 42
bridges, 15, 19, 20

CATIA, 26–29, 37
computer design, 26–29
contemporary art, 10

Euskadi, 11
exterior, 21, 29, 31–37

fashion shows, 6
foundation, 25–26, 29
framework, 29

galleries, 18, 41
Gehry, Frank Owen, 5–7, 13–15, 19–21, 26–27, 32, 40, 42
glass, 21, 31
Glymph, Jim, 26–27, 28

Guggenheim Foundation, 5–6, 10, 12, 15, 17, 18, 42
Guggenheim Museum Bilbao
 architects of, 21, 23–24
 construction of, 24–26
 cost of, 24, 29
 designing, 17–21
 economic impact of, 43
 exterior of, 21, 31–37
 foundation of, 25–26, 29
 framework of, 29
 galleries of, 18, 41
 opening of, 39, 41
 visitors of, 6, 41, 43

Huéscar quarry, 36–37, 43

IDOM, 23–24

Krens, Thomas, 12–13, 18, 41

limestone, 21, 28, 35–37

Nervión River, 13, 15, 25–26, 39

Puente de la Salve, 15, 18, 19, 20, 21, 41

skylights, 40
stainless steel, 31–32
steel, 21, 28, 29
stone, 35–37

titanium, 31–35
tourism, 5, 43

Vidarte, Juan Ignacio, 7, 40
visitors, 6, 41, 43

Wright, Frank Lloyd, 5–6

DISCARD